Questions for My Father

Questions

for

My Father

Finding the Man Behind Your Dad

Vincent Staniforth

ATRIA BOOKS
New York London Toronto Sydney

BEYOND WORDS
PUBLISHING

ATRIA BOOKS
A Division of Simon & Schuster, Inc.
1230 Avenue of the Americas
New York, NY 10020

20827 N.W. Cornell Road, Suite 500
Hillsboro, Oregon 97124-9808
503-531-8700 / 503-531-8773 fax
www.beyondword.com

Copyright © 1998, 2008 by Vincent Staniforth

Managing editor: Lindsay S. Brown
Editor: Marvin Moore
Cover and interior design: Richard Cohn, Fran Lee, and Sara E. Blum

First Atria Books/Beyond Words hardcover edition January 2008

ATRIA BOOKS and colophon are trademarks of Simon & Schuster, Inc.
Beyond Words Publishing is a division of Simon & Schuster, Inc.

For more information about special discounts for bulk purchases, please contact Simon & Schuster Special Sales at 1-800-456-6798 or business@simonandschuster.com.

Manufactured in the United States of America

10 9 8 7 6 5 4 3 2

Library of Congress Cataloging-in-Publication Data:

Staniforth, Vincent.
    Questions for my father : finding the man behind your dad /
Vincent Staniforth.

        p.   cm.
    1. Fathers and sons. I. Title.
    HQ756.S74 1998
    306.874'2—dc21   97-49136
                                                CIP

ISBN-13: 978-1-58270-244-5

The corporate mission of Beyond Words Publishing, Inc.: *Inspire to Integrity*

For

John Staniforth
and for my
sun and moon—
John Harley
and Conor David Edmund

Introduction

This book is the result of long midnight conversations with Dad—but they were conversations that took place in the dreams and quiet, troubled times in the years following his death. While I remember his answers to a few of these questions from his living years, for the rest I can only wish that he was around in person so I could hear his response without the unreliable filter of memory or interpretation.

This book may prompt dads and their children to ask each other these and many other questions. Or it may prompt dads to think of how their own fathers might have responded. But these are *my* questions, and by asking them I've recalled things Dad said and did that I would never have remembered had I not committed them to paper. While originally written with my own dad—and later, all dads—in mind, most of these questions can be addressed to both parents and can be asked by either a son or a daughter. The underlying objective, however, has been to develop a blueprint for discovery so that children of any age can build a clearer, deeper picture of the man behind the word *Dad*.

You could easily ask a set of questions completely different from mine, questions as urgent or as playful as those in the following pages. I was fortunate. I didn't have to ask any of the darker, angry questions that children sometimes have to ask; I assumed that all fathers were as constant and godlike as mine. Even so, Dad and I never talked about many of these questions and topics, and I don't want the same thing to happen to me and my sons. I want us to talk openly and deeply to each other—often—and I want to hear them ask many other questions, too.

I had ample opportunity to ask these questions, and the few times we talked candidly revealed in much more detail the beautiful man I knew my father was. Which makes my neglect of that relationship all the more painful. A million reasons not to ask these questions could always be found. It was a waste of all the things Dad had ever seen and done not to hear his answers, and I regret not finding out more about him when I had the chance.

So this is for my dad. And for all dads past, present, and future. And for their sons and daughters. And for the simple pleasure of talking to each other.

What's the most important
lesson you learned from your dad?

Who was your first love?

What's your biggest regret?

As a boy,
what did you want to be
when you grew up?

What was your happiest
teenage day?

Do you find yourself

saying

the same things to me

that your dad

said to you?

How did you learn about
the facts of life?

What's it like having

grown-up
children?

What does

God

mean to you?

It's important for children to allow their father to be seen as fallible, if only sometimes.

As a teenager, I felt I was immeasurably wiser and savvier than my dad. But as I grew older, I saw my dad as more of a man, because he let me share in some of his fears and regrets. Because of that courage in showing me that he was just another guy, I saw him even more as godlike and supremely lovable.

What's your secret for making
a woman smile?

Do you ever think about
your mom and dad?

Where and what do you think
I'll be when I'm seventy?

Do you ever think
about death?

I was talking with two old friends one evening about losing our fathers.

"We're part of a club," I said, "and everyone joins it sooner or later.

"We were lucky. We didn't have to subscribe till we were in our thirties. Some people join it from birth."

And so we raised our glasses to a toast of Making Every Second Count with our children.

How will I know when I've
met my true love?

Should I strive to be happy,
or strive to be successful?

What's the biggest mistake you've ever
made? What can I learn from it?

How should I deal
with hard times?

What makes a good dad?

What makes a good
son or daughter?

What happened on your
favorite holiday?

Have you ever regretted
having children?

How does a dad get through
his children's adolescence?

What has influenced and formed
your political thinking?

Are sports important?
How?

What's your favorite movie?

What did you feel
the first time
you cradled me
in your arms?

Should marriage really
mean *forever*?

Which is your favorite season?
Why?

Did you have to kill anyone
in the war?
Do you ever think about
those experiences?

A young man stands in the deep night of the jungle. He's at war, he's carrying a rifle, and he's scared.

Forty years later, another youth stands in a city with a checkbook in hand, just starting out in business, and scared.

Which one has more courage? I always thought that even if I lived through a dozen recessions, it still wouldn't be the same as having to go through a war like my dad. But he saw it differently, saying, "You're growing up in a different world. I wouldn't survive having to do what your generation has to do. They don't give out medals for getting up every morning and feeding a family.

"But that's what real guts is all about."

What's your favorite book? Why?

Where were you when man first set foot on the moon?

How would you feel if I wanted to be an artist or poet?

How did you deal
with your dad's death?

Coming to terms with my dad's death
did not come easily to me.
I once complained to my wife that it
just didn't seem fair that my dad had died
when I was only thirty.
    "I think you need to look at it another way,"
  she said. "You had him for thirty whole years."
    And the cloud vanished.
I saw myself as blessed, instead of
    unfairly treated.
Maybe we need to instill this viewpoint in our
children. Moms and dads are finite resources.
However long we have them needs to be
    the best time possible.
And I remember that comment
every time I pick up the phone
    to talk to Mom.

What did you always want
to do but never had the
chance?

What's your own
Golden Rule?

Questions to Ask My Children

What should it mean
when someone says,
"I love you"?

What's the biggest risk
you've ever taken?

How will I know when a risk
is worth taking?

What's the most important thing to
remember about money?

What did you want me to
be when I grew up?

What's the mark
of a good person?

Is mankind born
good or bad?

What do you love most
about this country?

If I'm in love with two women,
how do I know which to choose?

Can a man and a woman
find lasting happiness?

How hard should I pursue
my dreams?

What's the worst part
about growing older?

Life is unpredictable—
what's the best way
to handle its surprises?

What would your advice be
if I were drafted to go to war?

What's the biggest difference
between raising sons and daughters?

Which is more important
to study,
art or science?

What should I do when
someone wrongs me?

Is my life already determined,
or am I in control of my destiny?

Who has been your
best friend?

What makes a real friend?

I remember clearly, as do my
brother and sisters,
the delight we felt when our parents
used to tell us stories
about their childhood days.
What is it about imagining Dad
as a young boy that was so

mesmerising?

What's your most
vivid memory
of your mom and dad?

How will I know when
I'm successful?

Is it possible to be a complete adult without suffering hardship, adversity, or danger?

What do you believe happens
when we die?

In a world of compromises,
how do I keep true to myself?

What's the best part of
having a son?

Two minutes before a soccer match when I was seven, my bootlace snapped. While I fell apart, my dad calmly knelt and repaired the lace, softly saying, "Better it happened here than out on the field."

As young as I was, I thought it was a pretty amazing thing to say. As I grew up, I remember thinking how unlikely it would be that I would ever be as wise as my dad. Then, just recently, my own six-year-old son's bootlace snapped before a soccer game, and as I tied the lace while he fretted, I casually told him that it was better that this kind of thing happen on the sidelines rather than in the action. He agreed, and ran off happily to play his game.

As I watched, I realized that I'd just become conspirator in the Great Dad Pact—the secret game that all fathers play where we pretend to be the source of great wisdom that, in fact, we have merely inherited and made our own.

Is that so bad?
No, I think it's great that my sons, at this young age, can believe that whatever problems the world presents, Mom and Dad can fix them. There will be time enough in later years to see that it isn't so all the time. What I should have told him was that my dad did exactly the same thing for me and that it was all part of being a dad and of loving someone.

How will I know when I've found the
right place to put down roots?

What's the biggest
difference between my world
and the world you grew up in?

How did you propose to Mom?

What were the key events
that changed your life?

Where would you most like to
visit in the world?
Why?

What's the good part
about getting older?

How did it feel to let me go
to make my own life?

How can I make each
of my children feel as if
they're the most special?

How do I become

my own person

rather than the man

society says I should be?

Who do you admire the most?
Why?

Have you found it possible
to forgive people
who wronged you?

How will I know when to keep quiet
and when to speak my mind?

What do you think has been
your greatest achievement?

If you could go back and change
one event in your life,
what would it be
and how would you change it?

Is it better to be self-reliant
or to develop a network of friends
to call upon for help?

Do you think you're a
contented man?

What should I do when I'm angry
with my children?

I've learned so much from what I believe
my dad did right in his life.
I've also learned a lot from reflecting
   on the mistakes he made.
And when I get smug about being able to
develop my parent skills by learning
   from another's mistakes,
I suddenly realize that my boys will learn
from my mistakes.
                    Scary.

What did you like most—
and least—
about your dad?

Have you ever carried
a long-term grudge
against someone?
Why?

Have you ever had to do
something that took
a lot of courage?
What happened?

What was the funniest thing
you ever saw your children do?

Can you remember your parents
laughing? What was the cause?

What do you wish
you'd asked your dad?

Dads can be multidimensional
mystery characters.
Is it because they withhold so much,
or is it because
we don't ask the right questions?

Do you think you spent too much time at work when we were young?

Do you think you were too strict with your children?

Did you and Mom carefully plan how to raise us, or did you improvise?

If you could change
one thing about me,
what would it be?

What do you remember
about my character
as a young child?

What's your favorite
song of all time?
What or who does
it remind you of?

What's the best time of
life for a man?

What has been

your proudest day

as a dad?

Looking back through
your dad, granddad,
and so on,
what characteristic
do we all share?

What have you learned
from being a dad?

I'm not a perfect dad. I'm very far from it.
But I believe with all my heart that
I can be a better dad.
Can I be a better dad
than my own father?
We'll see—
but I'll do my best
to make sure that my children
will know me more completely
than I knew my dad,
and that's a start.

Have you kept secrets from
Mom during your marriage?
To protect you or her?

Have you ever
faced total despair?
What did you do?

What are your guiding
principles for doing business?

What were parties like
when you were
a young man?

What is a dad's primary
role—teacher, protector,
provider, pal, or disciplinarian?

How is my style of fatherhood
different from yours?

What do you think has been the
number one cause of our arguments?

What makes
a good daughter?

Do you fear more for
a son or a daughter
as they face
the outside world?

How have you wanted
your children
to think of you?

How do you ask these questions without
     creating an awkward moment?
     Maybe that's the problem.
We've gotten out of the habit of having
     meaningful conversations.
One of the casualties of our time is that the
     people who should matter the most
     are the ones we often take for granted.

Did you ever feel complete anger
and frustration at your children?
How did you deal with it?

How does the role of
a dad and a mom differ?

What would you change
about your style of fathering?

How did you and Mom keep
your relationship alive
while raising a family?

Did you enjoy
being single?

Who first broke your heart?
What happened?

What makes you proud
to be a man?

Does a man "love" differently
than a woman?

*I*s there such a thing as
a "right" war?

*A*ll things considered,
would you rather have grown up
in your world or
in today's world?

Did being a dad come naturally?

What causes racial
or religious prejudice?

What makes a good
spouse?

Are you frightened
of anything now?

Is there anything you've
always wanted to ask me?

How old do you feel today?

Should I live
with my mistakes or always
try to cut my losses and
make a clean start?

Did your parents have
favorites? Did you?

If you were a young man today,
would you have a family again?

Define *family*.

Define *a life well lived.*

What's the best part of
having a daughter?

When I was born,
what was your
dream for me?

Questions to Ask My Dad

What are the vital

ingredients of

a strong marriage?

What's
your favorite memory
of spending time with me?

What did you worry
about most as
I was growing up?

How did you meet Mom?
Where did you go
on your first date?

How long did you know each
other before you got married?

What was your
wedding day like?

What would you do if something happened to Mom?

What did you always want
to do with your kids
but never had the chance?

Were you ever tempted to
just walk away from your
family responsibilities?

How have you remotivated yourself when faced with bad times?

What was the greatest
gift your parents gave
you? Have you tried to
instill the same lessons
in your children?
Do you think
you succeeded?

Should I try to retain
an idealistic worldview
or adopt
a more pragmatic view?

When did you get your first car?
What model was it?

Did you go as far
academically
as you wanted?

What was your
happiest school day?

What was your first job?

When you were

growing up,
did you hope to be a
father someday?

Afterword

These questions should have been asked when Dad was alive. They remained unasked for many reasons: lack of time, lack of nerve in some cases (*Will he be offended if I ask him this question?*), lack of courage in others (*Do I really want to know the answer to that question?*). But they remained lodged in my head because of a fierce desire, growing stronger as I matured (slowly), to know—truly know—my dad. For me, as I suspect is the case with many men and women, that desire for knowledge seemed to burn brightest just before the extinction of the source of its energy. My realization of how much more I wanted to learn about my dad came so clearly that I can still recall the moment.

It's a rainy afternoon in Telluride, Colorado, in mid-September 1990. A married man of nearly three weeks, I am honey-mooning on a cross-country motorcycle trip from Atlanta to San Francisco. Ominous, piling clouds have been chasing us down these mountain roads all morning. Cold and wet, we decide to stop in this town for the night and revive ourselves with coffee and brandy at a bar on the main street.

Viv, my wife, goes exploring while I order another brandy with hot water and mull over the notes I've been making since we left Atlanta. These scribbles are comments on what we've seen, the people we've met, the minor hitches and laughs that make up any travelogue, but I begin to notice that as we've travelled farther down the road, my notes are becoming more abstract, less literal. My notes talk about how it feels to be married (no surprise there), and I imagine how Mom and Dad started their life together in 1947; I comment on the enormity and uncertainty of this bike ride—we're a long way from our home in England—and try to imagine how Dad thought about his own long journey as an infantryman in Burma in World War II.

Taking my pen, I begin to write; I ask myself to imagine what it must have been like for my parents to let me go and begin to live my own life. On another motorcycle, on another rainy day a long time ago, I see Dad waving from the kitchen window as I leave to ride to college. How did that feel for him? Then I ask them what it's like having grown-up children. I wish more than anything else that Dad was beside me at this bar so we could talk and talk and he could tell me much more about who he is.

According to my watch, it's 2:30 p.m. Mountain Time, which puts England at 9:30 p.m. A map of the United States hangs over the breakfast bar of my parents' kitchen, and not for the first time during this ride I become very sure that right now he's looking at the map and tracing our route, wondering if we're safe, and looking forward to our return. Looking in the mirror behind the bar in Telluride, I get the eerie but not uncomfortable feeling that Dad is looking back at me from the other side. I wish he were here. I have a terrible feeling of time slipping through my fingers.

Ten days later, back in Atlanta and getting ready to fly home to England, I took a call telling me that Dad had had a stroke. The next day, jet-lagged and disbelieving, I sat next to him as he fought the stroke that had taken his consciousness and was relentlessly battering him toward death. The youngest of his five children sharing the long hours of vigil, I sat alone with him in the empty hours of the morning and recounted events from the motorcycle trip in the hope that he could still hear and understand a familiar voice. Stories poured out of me about our adventures and the times I'd thought so vividly about him in places like Memphis, Boulder, the Grand Canyon, Telluride, and Big Sur. But Dad was unconscious and gave no sign of recognition beyond a small flicker of his fingers when I first held his hand. He died a couple of hours later.

In the years following his death, I came to see just how much I had failed to learn from

Dad—and about Dad. Certainly, he'd bestowed upon me the broad strokes, the crucial guidelines and directives that shaped me and continue to shape me—and my two sons— even today. I knew I was loved. He knew I loved him. But there was so much more there. All that time, all I ever had to do was ask the questions. But they remained unasked, and so all I have today is memory, conjecture, interpretation, and a determination that my children won't know this kind of frustration. So the questions and ideas that Dad and I addressed in my dreams and in those solitary, quiet moments were put to paper. Over time, the list grew and grew. It was therapy, a way of coping with his death. It was good to talk to Dad again.

One day in 1996, I was sitting in a bagel shop, laboring over an early draft of this book, when two women noticed the papers spread out before me and asked what the questions were about. After I explained the idea behind the book, one of them exclaimed, "Oh, neat!" and began leafing through a couple of pages. The second woman said, "You know, I'd use this to start talking to my dad. All we do is argue. I can just sit him down at Thanksgiving and start asking him this stuff." The first woman put the sheaf of papers back on the table and added, "But where are the answers?" I replied that I'd been asking the same question since my dad died. After they left, her comment echoed again and again, giving me doubts about the whole project. Why, I asked myself, in a culture that spoonfeeds information and products to consumers each and every day, would anyone be interested in reading a stream of questions without having recourse to an index of answers? I almost left that draft in the trash can.

Instead, the book continued to develop, and gradually I saw the woman's question as the absolute essence of why the book needed to see publication. The very fact that there are no answers within these covers focuses the reader on the questions. No one can repeat any question to themselves without formulating some kind of reply, however abstract or abrupt. There was a need, I believed, to put such questions down on paper and use them as a blueprint to uncover more about the man behind the word *Dad*.

My encounter with the women in the bagel shop also made me see the book in another light; so far, I'd been approaching the idea from my own particular circumstance, i.e., my dad had died and these were questions that I wished I had asked him when he was still alive. But what about those people who want to learn more about their fathers who are still living? What about fathers who want to talk about these questions and issues, unbidden, to their children? What about children who want to know more about their father's relationship with his father? The book seemed to be offering a proto-map of discovery not only of the father figure but also of the reader. It was offering a way—sometimes playful, sometimes serious—to let fathers tell their stories and to make children, young or old, explore their own knowledge and understanding of their dad. And if that knowledge and understanding simply does not exist—for whatever reason—the questions then turn around and shine an inquiring light onto the reader: *How do I think my dad might have answered this question? How do I think I might answer the same question to my children?*

Considering these questions, you might come to agree with the view that this book is more about self-discovery than dad-discovery. And finally, I want to emphasize that these are my questions. I urge you to develop your own questions. Sit down with your dad—even if he's not around—and ask him your questions. Sit down with your children and answer the same questions. Make your own discovery. We have to stop being afraid of asking questions. And we have to start being brave enough to listen to the answers.

Notes

Notes

The Secret

Author: Rhonda Byrne

$23.95, hardcover

As seen on Oprah, the groundbreaking feature-length movie that revealed the great mystery of the universe, *The Secret*, is now a book, and everything you have ever wanted—unlimited joy, health, money, relationships, love, youth—is now at your very fingertips.

The Secret is an enigma that has existed throughout the history of mankind. It has been discovered, coveted, suppressed, hidden, lost, and recovered. Now for the first time The Secret is revealed to the world between the covers of this captivating book. In it you'll find all the resources you will ever need to understand and live The Secret. The book shares amazing real-life stories and testimonials of regular people who have changed their lives in profound ways. *The Secret* offers guidance on how to apply this powerful knowledge to your life in every area from health to wealth, to success and relationships, so you can obtain everything you've always wanted. No matter who you are, no matter where you are right now, no matter what you want—when you realize The Secret you can have anything.

The Power of Appreciation:
The Key to a Vibrant Life
Authors: Noelle C. Nelson, Ph.D. and Jeannine Lemare Calaba, Psy.D.
$14.95, softcover
Research confirms that when people feel appreciation, good things happen to their minds, hearts, and bodies. But appreciation is much more than a feel-good mantra. It is an actual force, an energy that can be harnessed and used to transform our daily life—relationships, work, health and aging, finances, crises, and more. *The Power of Appreciation* will open your eyes to the fabulous rewards of conscious, proactive appreciation. Based on a five-step approach to developing an appreciative

mind-set, this handbook for living healthier and happier also includes tips for overcoming resistance and roadblocks, research supporting the positive effects of appreciation, and guidelines for creating an Appreciators Group.

The Art of Thank You:
Crafting Notes of Gratitude
Author: Connie Leas
$14.95, hardcover
While reminding us that a little gratitude can go a long way, this book distills the how-tos of thank-yous. Part inspirational, part how-to, *The Art of Thank You* will rekindle the gratitude in all of us and inspire readers to pick up a pen and take the time to show thanks. It stresses the healing power that comes from both giving and receiving thanks and provides practical, concrete, and inspirational examples of when to write a thank-you note and what that notes should include. With its appealing and approachable style, beautiful gift presentations, charming examples, and real-life anecdotes, *The Art of Thank You* has the power to galvanize readers' resolve to start writing their all-important thank-you notes.

A Guy's Guide to Pregnancy:
Preparing for Parenthood Together
Author: Frank Mungeam
$12.95, softcover

Every day, four thousand American men become first-time dads. There are literally hundreds of pregnancy guide-books aimed at women, but guys rarely rate more than a footnote. *A Guy's Guide to Pregnancy* is the first book to explain in "guy terms" the changes that happen to a guy's partner and their relationship during pregnancy, using a humorous yet insightful approach.

Teach Only Love:
The Twelve Principles of Attitudinal Healing
Author: Gerald G. Jampolsky, M.D.
$12.95, softcover

The concept of attitudinal healing has become even more popular ever since Dr. Jampolsky first published this paradigm-shifting book sixteen years ago. His work has resonated with readers; his practical, yet endearing perspective can help everyone learn to unconditionally love someone in their life: parents, children, spouses, friends, and even coworkers.

Teach Only Love also helps readers learn to love themselves. There is another way to move through this world without resorting to fear or the emotional battles people push themselves through each day. Readers can experience peace and a mental and spiritual balance that will hold steady no matter what occurs in day-to-day circumstances. The principles in *Teach Only Love* can retrain the mind to perceive its own freedom and find total acceptance—without boundaries or expectations.

Notes from the Universe:
Book One
Author: Mike Dooley
$17.95, hardcover

The secret to manifesting change is not focusing on the *how*, but rather the end result of what readers are after—the kind of life *they* want. Then, once they are truly focused, the Universe will conspire on their behalf.

Mike Dooley has turned over every stone, knocked on every door, and followed every impulse. From these lessons he learned, Dooley was able to share the Universe's wisdom with the world. What started in 1998 as a little poem sent out once a week to thirty-eight email addresses has evolved into an inspiring anecdote delivered to more than 100,000 subscribers from 169 countries, each receiving a new note from the Universe, five days a week.

Notes from the Universe begins a three-volume set that is brimming with powerful affirmations that will have readers thinking positively, feeling confident, and walking the path to personal success.

Watermelon Magic:
Seeds of Wisdom, Slices of Life
Author: Wally Amos
$14.95, softcover
Watermelon Magic is an inspirational/motivational book using watermelons as a metaphor for life. Utilizing the life experiences of Wally Amos, the book shows the parallels between watermelons and humans. Watermelon Magic tells how Wally Amos uses his faith in everyday life and the wisdom gained from the past to help him make wise choices. Just as the vine connects the watermelons, we are all connected by spirit. And just as prickly vines make it difficult to get the melons, our human connections are sometimes prickly, making it

difficult for us to achieve our goals and realize our dreams. *Watermelon Magic* helps us acknowledge the difficulties and choose a path to success.

Home Sweeter Home:
Creating a Haven of Simplicity and Spirit
Author: Jann Mitchell; Foreword: Jack Canfield
$12.95, softcover
We search the world for spirituality and peace— only to discover that happiness and satisfaction are not found "out there" in the world but right here in our houses and in our hearts. Award-winning journalist and author Jann Mitchell offers creative insights and suggestions for making our home life more nurturing, spiritual, and rewarding for ourselves, our families, and our friends.

Little Wave and Old Swell:
A Fable of Life and Its Passing
Author: Jim Ballard
$16.95, hardcover
In this simple and engaging parable, author Jim Ballard recounts a journey across the sea made by young and impetuous Little Wave and his sagacious teacher, Old

Swell. Their metaphorical adventures point readers and listeners alike towards the age-old questions: *Where did I come from? What is the nature of life? What happens when I die?* Inspired by the teaching of Paramahansa Yogananda—bestselling author of *Autobiography of a Yogi*—*Little Wave and Old Swell* is an ideal gift book that includes original oil paintings by Catherine M. Elliott and a foreword by Kenneth Blanchard, business guru and bestselling author of *The One Minute Manager*.

To order or to request a catalog, contact
BEYOND WORDS PUBLISHING, INC.
20827 N.W. Cornell Road, Suite 500
Hillsboro, OR 97124-9808
503-531-8700
www.beyondword.com

BEYOND WORDS

P U B L I S H I N G

Our corporate mission:

Inspire to Integrity

Our declared values:

We give to all of life as life has given us.

We honor all relationships.

Trust and stewardship are integral
to fulfilling dreams.

Collaboration is essential to create miracles.

Creativity and aesthetics nourish the soul.

Unlimited thinking is fundamental.

Living your passion is vital.

Joy and humor open our hearts to growth.

It is important to remind ourselves of love.

Printed in the United States
By Bookmasters